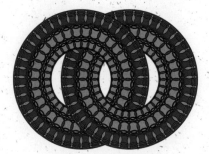

BEAR

BEAR

KAREN CHASE

poetry

CavanKerry ◈ Press LTD.

CavanKerry Press Ltd.
Fort Lee, New Jersey
www.cavankerrypress.org

Library of Congress Cataloging-in-Publication Data

Chase, Karen Block
Bear / Karen Chase. – 1st ed.
p. cm.
ISBN-13: 978-1-933880-06-8
ISBN-10: 1-933880-06-6
1. Bears–Poetry. I. Title.

PS3553.H33464B43 2008
811'.54–dc22

20070388370C.

Cover art, James O'Brien © 2007
Author photograph by Ogden Gigli
Cover and book design by Peter Cusack

First Edition 2008
Printed in the United States of America

NOTABLE ◈ VOICES

CavanKerry Press is proud to publish the works
of established poets of merit and distinction.

CavanKerry Press is grateful for the support it
receives from the New Jersey State Council on the Arts.

For Paul

Acknowledgments

Grateful acknowledgment is made to the editors of the following publications in which these poems first appeared, some in slightly different form:

Alaska Quarterly Review: "Grid"
Agni (Online): "Mercury"
Another Chicago Magazine (ACM): "End of My First Marriage"
The Berkshire Review: "Sanatorio Serbelloni"
Exquisite Corpse: "Sayings"
Hotel Amerika: "Striper"
Poet Lore: "A Glistening"
Poetry Ireland: "The Cradle"
The Southern Review: "Food For Thought," "Contemporariness"
upstreet: "Arranging Books as Elegy," "Throwing Away Books," "Dusk in the South," "The Angel of Used Things"

"Beach Rubble" appears in *The Breath of Parted Lips: Voices from the Robert Frost Place, Volume 2* (CavanKerry Press, 2004)

Special thanks to my dear friends and poets Jeffrey Harrison and Didi Goldenhar. Thanks to Barbara and Norty Garber, Jessica Greenbaum, Londa Weisman, Joan Handler, and Trudy Ames. Much gratitude to the Macdowell Colony for time to work on these poems, and to Lieutenant Tom Kazprzak who educated me in the ways of bears.

Contents

A Glistening

Along a shore
of sand formation
like vanished
civilization
we are going
for dorados.
From turquoise waves
Paul pulls one in.
The fish gleams gold
hits the air—blink—
the gold's gone.

A Glistening

Jam

Our love is not the short
courtly kind but
upstream, down,
long inside—enjambed,
enjoined, conjoined, and
jammed, it's you, enkindler,
enlarger, jampacked man of many
stanzas, my enheartener—love
runs on from line to
you, from line to me and me
to you, from river to sea and sea to
land, hits a careless coast, meanders
way across the globe—land
ahoy! water ahoy!—love
with no end, my waters go
wherever you are, my stream
of consciousness.

Striper

We woke to a blowing gray
sky, whitecaps spraying our
shack, tide lashing in, we made a

lot of love the day and night before
as sun and blue turned to
dark, as clouds flew

from left to right. We slid open
the glass door, wind pushed through
the room, salt settling everywhere.

As waves broke over his torso, a man
at the end of the pilings hauled in
stripers. The bay rose. Paul made his way

down the beach to see if he'd sell us a fish.
"Hell no!" the man yelled above the wind.
"Want one? Take this."

Paul ran back to the shack, flapping
fish in hand. I ran out with board and knife
and Paul began, as he knelt in the blowing sand,

to make the first large cut. Blood
splat over sand and board, red
covered his hands.

Sex and paint, I thought, how blood was
part of how we loved, how each month
it came to my life for us both.

As tide covered the pilings, the wind
died down. Then we packed up our fish
and headed for home.

Food for Thought

I've caught fish, sorry to brag,
been ecstatic with their size—
a twenty-pound salmon,
a *gallo* taller than my height—
cod, blues, a *cierra*, a large striped bass, trout,
to name a few.

In the morning dark in the Sea of Cortés
we saw silhouettes as we motored out.
And bones of a man the day before
were in a little museum
on a bed of snails in sand,
vertebrae in a design, the skull to the right.

Today though, we were fishing from a *panga*,
slightly larger than a rowboat.
Were the waves big?
I found out later—apparently not.
They seemed huge.
The boat bonked loud on each one.

Later the captain unfurled the canvas top,
a shield from the rising sun.
A troop of spiders crawled out.
He jumped back for a wooden pincer,
plucked and tossed them one by one.

What a relief
to see the captain's red brown skin
and I sure looked.

When he bent, his jeans slid down—
you could see how his back became his behind.

Chumming, he dug his hand into some red bonito flesh,
threw chunks into the sea, and for once I understood—
it's not easy to have a woman on a boat.

The Cradle

Copper and gold skittering off, glinting stroke and wash,
sweep of paint ignoring the frame.
In the center, a bison.

Like blood, color abounds in this field,
colostrum, meconium—the palette has changed.
The painter had visited Lascaux Cave.

The bison stamps its hooves.
The field reels off the wall, its flow grows larger,
the canvas seethes so new, a baby gets born. *Baby,*
what was it like rushing into the light?

When the painter was asked what it was like
living in the shadow of her husband—swish of paint—
"I've never been in his shadow. I stood in his light."

A beast stands on the savanna, stares down the frame.
Another horse in hues of red hurries to reach the edge.
A horse, steady at the bottom, eyes the outstretched plain.

Dusk in the South

Low odor of tide
as we canoe through
the mangroves.

From purplish water,
roots emerge like feet
of god knows what beast.

We are discussing
the courts and crime—
a snowy egret flies by.

The sky goes from grey to greyer,
stars unshingle the moon,
shrapnel smell invades the tide,
the vegetable world turns animal.

Beach Rubble

I love nature, said Paul, having walked the jetty
past the breakwater, tide fast filling in below us.
Thus began our long walk across the dunes to get back.
"Did you say *like* or *love*?" I asked.

He is saying, "That looks like bittersweet but it's not"

and ". . . undulating grass . . ."

He shook rope from a bollixed net,
"good piece of rope," he said,
examined a flowerpot "good pot."
When he picked up a glove, I knew what he thought.

Traipsing towards the mainland through the dunes,
I thought of Jane and Flicka hiking in the sand
when the car hit, the driver asleep.
Later, my son found all that was left—
their sunscreen and walking stick.

In the dizzy light of this beach, I saw Paul
pick a plastic bottle out
from the sand. It looked like praying.

Bear, I Need You

Traditional Alutiiq address before the hunt begins

Bear Safety

From The Bear Safety Pamphlet—
Do not run.
Let the bear know you are not prey.
Act human, wave your arms.
Speak to the bear.

Are you scared,
Bear? Does my smell
cause your fur to curdle?
You make my skin crawl.

Do my English words
worry you? Can you feel
my breath, Bear? Do you
worry, Bear, who's in charge?
Sometimes you go too far.
I am thirsty

for your burgundy meat.
What do you think?
You'd eat me, Bear, and I,
I would eat you. And you?
What is it you want?
My skin is white and smooth.

I do not belong
in this far north town

where there are tales
of men and bear who marry.
I'd never live near
the allusive luscious
sea with you.

Stand on your
hind legs, Bear, and I
will stand on mine, let's
face each other down.

Traveling in Bear Country

Are you listening, Bear?
I am speaking to you!
Are you afraid?
I dream I'm stalking you—
do I confuse you, Bear?—
I'm wearing fur, eating berries.

You and I, Bear, we feel
sun warm the air.
In the underbrush once,
it shone the yellows van Gogh used.
You don't even know who van Gogh was.

I once read, Bear,
that you know when a human
is carrying a gun. You sense
our arrogance and then you attack
out of fear, from aggression
because you sense ours.

Bear, I have a confession.
I want to learn to shoot.
Indulge me—how small
I feel in the face of you.

I look down at the ground,
at the tiny yellow cinquefoils,
at the campions, the cotton grass,
I look out to the great white massifs,

over to the exploding river, gunmetal
grey from glaciers, out at the green
tundra where you wander unnamed streams.
Bear, I belong back in my yard, worrying
about words and money, acting human.

The Hint

The bear safety pamphlet says:
act human, wave your arms,
speak to the bear,
but I have nothing more to say to you.

Just because I can speak, Bear, don't
expect me to. It's not always human
to talk, in case you didn't know.

Sometimes we'd rather act—
you know about that.
The skewed way you glance sideways

at an armed man gets fear across
better than talking can. Don't take
your chances with me, Bear—

you are stronger but we are smarter.
Right now I am using my brain as you
sleep in your den. Hint:
we gain advantage with tools.

Don't fool with me. I hear stories
from friends who know your kind.

Today, Bear, I am having laser surgery,

on my bum right thumb, to fix,
you should excuse the expression,
a trigger thumb which
goes out of joint, pops.

What the safety pamphlet had in mind when
it advised hikers to speak to the bear
and act human was not this I am sure,
but for your information,

humans talk a lot
about their ailments.

Ursa Major

If I were addressing humans
I would tend to speak to him or
to him or him over there.
I would not speak

to our whole species all
at once, so I regret, Bear,
talking to you in general.
As I just looked at a chart

of mammal tracks, yours are
the ones that look footlike.
Bear, who are you? I keep hearing
tales: the one who snatched a baby

from her stroller into the woods,
the bear with stinking offal breath,
and the scared bear treed
in the maple down my street.

Bear, you, like snowflakes,
you, like us and like stars in the sky—
each different is what's the same—
I love how you make the Big Dipper shine.

Hunting

Today, Bear, I learned something
new—the Bering Strait
is the only boundary between
Chukotka, Russia, and Alaska.
Point: humans hunt in more ways
than one. We set out into
the forest, going for another
kind of food. That's how
I bagged this fact.

More to the point for you, Bear,
is this: some humans of Chukotka
believe bears understand their
local languages, particularly
Koryak, and, if spoken to gently,
humans can come to agreements
with them. But, the humans say,
the Tang language irritates the bears.
So this is just to say, I hope
English agrees with you.

More Hunting the Dark Woods of Knowledge

Today, Bear, I brought this back—
the Alutiiqs of Kodiak hunted
bear and ate their, rather *your*,
meat and fat—they used your
sinew for thread and your teeth
as jewels. At night, they
wrapped your lush fur
around themselves
as they slept. Dreaming—

I once told you I'd never
live—this I say as a
sleepwalker—near
the sea with you—
remember? It had to
do with tales
of men and bear who
marry. The more
I know you though, the more
I hunt these
tangled woods, the
more I'm not so sure.

Inside the Lockup

Stuck

The stories in this lockup
suck—the past raked up
like jittery garbage—nothing

turned to anything useful, like
dirt, I mean. The artifacts stink.
There's no getting out—not you,
and what's worse, not me.

The Book of Crime

Cooped up men in jail
for sin or worse, I have turned
away from their words.

In my own cell now,
picturing wind keeps me
from sleep. How much
I would barter for one single breeze.

•

Doing Time

Each night I empty crates of books
and bones, the price I pay for crime.
Still, I'm not sorry for what

I've done. Was I wrong for learning
to shoot? Was I wrong for carrying a
gun? Or is it because I have spent
my time doing nothing called useful.

Unpacking

Single edge razor, box cutter,
knife—each appended as finger.
I dream of Struwwelpeter. I used

to write, I used to love cardboard. But
now I cut, untape, rip. Onto the floor
I throw this or that, yearn for dull
tools—pens, spoons.

It's Dusk

And you are innocent in a field, admiring the plump
gray light, the katydids, then you walk towards
the woods, hesitate—how dark it looks. Once in there,

fear departs as we all do, which gets me to this: why
exactly do we make such a deal of causing another's death?
Be it the one-time murderer in the next cell, or even
those who kill and kill. Death, anyway, comes on

us all, no matter what.
Every live second counts, that is why.
It had rained so much, the forest floor filled with
mushrooms of every color, every degree of newness or decay

and because I have landed behind bars, I now have nothing
to lose. So I sampled them all and am alive to tell the
tale. Do not always believe what you hear
about what is dangerous and what is not.

And Then I Saw a Salamander

When you make a loud sound, the guards
bring out the handcuffs, stuff a gag
up your throat.
I have got to get out.

I want to go to the range to shoot,
aim at the distant paper target.
Bullets mark it, as words on a page do.

Dark woods—bull's-eye—words are one exit
from this booby hatch. See there
on the mute ground—see the wiggling
salamander, looking for a way out too.

Then I Talked to a Bear

Bear, you are all the people
I have ever lost and all those
I dread losing, who knows the order.

In this house of lost ones, you are my
soulmate, a word I never used. This prison
has stolen my subjunctives, my roar and
lungs—think if a hunter cut your tongue.

Alternatives

Am I going to rot in this place, Bear,
mired in this gummed-up swamp of loss?
I am starting to count worse ways

to go and there are mighty few.
Maul me on the tundra, I don't
care. At least my last gulp
will be full of fresh air.

The Tundra

The tundra, the taiga, Bear, I am
desparate for space, take me there,
I abhor this chitchat place.
Hunter, here's my tongue—
the trophy's yours.

As long as I make noise
from my body deep,
that is all I care for.
And for this, Bear, to leave here,
I'll do anything you please.

Grid

The Abandoned Briggs Marble Quarry

Imperfect rectangles
marked by drill line,
slabs in the woods
slant in disorder,
upright, horizontal.

Fallible to earth's
black dust, stained
by juniper berry,
it takes the sledge
to reveal your white slice.

We are orphans to these stones,
soft and impressioned by song,
flawed by weather.

While you push outward,
weighty creatures in stone,
we write poems to attain mass.

Holy Wall

When you asked if
I felt closed in and
yes I said, pacing
the perimeter of
the abbey walls, wanting
to scale them to
get out or in, out
to town or in to see your
cloistered ways behind
your walls, and when you
said, "In these walls there's
nowhere to go but
up," I did not think of God.

I thought of birds and
their luck, how they rise
from my side of the
wall, land on your
catalpa.

Sayings

I have what I call my "polio pack," an old suitcase with
mail that came when I was sick. I found an envelope with
SAYINGS scrawled in turquoise ink across its front. In bed,
for fun, I must have cut scraps of words out.

Over six feet tall, muscularly built, with the brawn,
stamina and power of an all-American footballer

(FDR before he was struck?
A boy I liked?)

My Stomach's Empty

(Dough, I think now or thought)

Men of Science

(My father the food chemist?
Jonas Salk?)

Every Saturday when I was a girl, the UPS man came with a
large package my father ripped apart. Doughnut boxes
stacked on the maroon marbled linoleum.

My father got his yellow pad out, opened each box, took
a bite from a doughnut—chewed, paused, made notes, then
spit the mouthful out.

For years I loved eating raw dough.
I'd make a batch with butter and flour when I was low.

All the girls are batty over Daddy-o

He'd take me crabbing in our rowboat. There's a photo
of FDR alone in one. You can tell it's hot. He's pulled
his trousers up, so his thinned legs, brace-covered, show.
He's fishing. I've fished so much.

How history
happens in photos,
Jonas Salk
in a white lab coat
gazing down the camera's throat, or
one of my father
garbed too in lab whites, staring
through the lens.

When I got sick,
and couldn't walk,
a photo
of me in Sunshine Cottage,
the polio ward.

I'm standing, it's January, I don't know what had hit,
I'm leaning,
leaning

like a photo of FDR against a bed,
hands gripping hard,
balancing me/him/us
up.
As if, what?

Our knuckles are white.

He's smiling
as one hand steadies,
the other waves.
I'm little.
My face is strained.

What place has the camera here?

I just wanted to walk.

Three months after the photo of me leaning,
we heard on the radio
Jonas Salk
made the vaccine.

National Relief

*

A snapshot of me in braids.
It's braidlike,
how me and everyone else
interweave.

Take water.

From Warm Springs, Georgia, they sent me stuff about FDR,
a bad xerox of him in water—it looks like it was stuck
in a drawer.

I rexeroxed it
onto onion skin,
it's texture thin.
Writing now, I just pinned it
over my desk,
got nervous,
paced, couldn't breathe, what to say now?
I forget.

Water.
Photo.
History.
Intersect.

Just his little face shows.

*

Underwater his legs are causing very small ripples.

He looks distant.

Water is holding him up.

Before he got sick he had been fishing from a small boat,
slipped overboard, "I'd never felt anything so cold.

It seemed paralyzing, the icy shock."
Then the forest fire he fought—Campobello, exhaustion, chills,
"lumbago," he thought.

Next day,
"When I swung
out of bed
my left leg
lagged,
but
I managed to move about
to shave."

His thumb muscles
got so weak
he couldn't write.

I too
was photographed
in water
—same ripples across the photo—but
my face gleaming,
my hair, loose,
streams in the onion skin waves.

Don't Fence Me In

Juvenile Delinq

The War Is Over

Sayings I cut out say.

Grid

What are you putting in your mouth
you wonder one day as you lick a stamp.
What are you putting on your skin, what
are you breathing in? When did history start?
Dancers do positions one and two

in pink satin ballet shoes,
then pray on their knees.
Straus composes a waltz.
Time's mixed up above and beneath.
German planes drop maps of France

dotted with swastikas, drumming
fear into the English countryside.
"You are surrounded. Throw down your arms."
Leaflets drift down in history's whirlwind,
the helix goes round.
Today I hear a plane—*plane!*—

the word suddenly changed.
The pearlized sky is not natural,
nor is the ruby-washed sea.
I'm scared of fresh ruins.
Hopping on a plane, to love—what a luxury

that was—the dry Mayan ruins of Uxmal,
or Palenque, under the wraps of jungle.
The stagnant pond where sacrifices were made,
jewels buried in the black muck still.

Anghor Selinute Macchu Picchu Tikal—
to love fragments is no good now,
to let the mind roll free.
Nightfall has fluttered down
into graves that are stories deep.

Who's that little girl? All she wants
is to sprawl about on the grass.
All she wants is to curl up on the couch.
Suddenly thick clouds arrive.
But it's just weather.
Wind corkscrews up like a helix, sucks fish
from the ocean, then drops the silver slivers down.
The ground's in grand confusion.
The wind

or mind—
is it blowing now?
The mind blows the trees down,
knocks over manmade structures.
Crows caw through the yellowlit sky,
every birch rises blue and skyward—
a lash of red ribbons—flags slice the skyline,
eagles screech towards the light.

Me and my shadow stretch one finger out straight,
an effort so enormous, all that comes to mind
is nuclear reaction. In wormbound sadness, people
who disdain prayer hold up their palms.

Sides of buildings wear away and patterns begin.
The start of the past?

Land and home of the free and the brave,
the Cockpit of Europe, the Land of Regrets,
Bogland, Motherland, Land of the Midnight Sun.
The confused land the day maps fell on English fields,
the day fish fell from the sky, the day planes
hit the towers. Everything flew down in the wind
and broken glass, the grid of history, landed in Brooklyn.

No Noise Now

You sleep through
the dark   dawn
is nothing   you
sleep through the day
you sleep through
winter   through
summer too   you sleep
through bells tolling
reds greens blues

End of My First Marriage

Tops of the trees blew yesterday back
and forth. The maple wagged warm
in the air as if before
a hurricane, and a willow
rocked like mad,
roots tearing from the ground.
To call it weather did not do.

Tonight we will leave
our hilltop, walk down the steep
pavement with no idea
what's in store. It's late winter or
is it—moon of the snowblind—

we open the kitchen door,
go out the screened-in porch
onto the street. We make jokes,
head straight down towards lights
of the town, which we will never make.
My husband slows his pace,

stretches his long lanky frame out
on the yellow divider line,
settles on the blacktop,
his eyes on heaven.
No-one says anything.

Sea Ballad

We're in trouble big trouble said
Captain Dave as he ran down from

his high perch. Full day
Gulf Stream fishing, going for

amberjack. A siren went off.
All the men stayed calm. Klein,

from pills against seasickness, stayed
asleep. I tried to calm down too.

The captain and mate ran around
trying things as the smell of gas

floated on us all. The good-looking
guy from New Mexico made jokes about napalm.

No way to get the motor to go.
Out to sea 9 miles and waves slapping the

boat as we rock and roll and the men
make jokes. I make one then puke,

notice Drum Stick is the name
of the boat and do it again. One by one the men

get quiet. When Paul takes a newspaper from his pack,
"Are you a former astronaut?"

the barfing teenage son of the New Mexican asks.
Finally, I ask

could the Coast Guard come get us?
"They don't rescue people for seasickness,"

the mate replies. "Only for something serious."
We had passed the place where Blackbeard

was beheaded. He had braided his beard,
tied the braids with red ribbons.

When his head was cut off
his body swam around like a chicken's.

The victors tied his head to their bowsprit
so good over evil ruled the sea.

Time passed. Some men on the boat got sicker.
Klein continued to sleep. Paul continued to read.

As the woman on the boat, I
was the designated sissy, I came to understand—

I had been put there to puke first
and worry out loud.

The grateful puking men liked me a lot.
Miss Kathleen arrived, towed us back.

And there was nary a sign of pirate in that deep rolling black.

Sanatorio Serbelloni

A girl launders our sheets each day,
runs the mangle and a boy walks
newspapers up the hill. Sometimes I walk

down to the lake, watch fish
scavenge the edge,
cavedonno they call them.

Air blows and blows on
the nearby hills of Pescallo.
Warblers fly level to my window.

Singing with my chums,
homey voices around the piano,
the furniture wildly shiny.

Everyone in the rain, we go out, our white
umbrellas wooden-handled. Swallows
do not keep up their intense flight.

Windblown boats skim the lake.
Walking in the gardens, a long sound
snakes over the ground.

Cherries drop across the road.
Blue salvia everywhere—two days ago
Italian snows steamed into a mountain town.

Sometimes my friends and I spend time, try
to decipher night's agitation
or we just forget it.

The sky turns black under the sword
of evening where it's hard
to get geography right.

I imagine Alps off to the west, snow
I think, is falling on them.
I, though, am fine now.

Sheets, ironed and white, make cotton
on my skin all right. The maid Vittoria
turned my sheets down before I

went back to my room. She put out a new
bottle of agua minerale, and cookies too.
Bed sores—the ward—when I was young.

In the lit arch by my window, she, earlier,
had placed wildflowers in a vase.
A cat below meows near the cypresses.

Townspeople down by the Lake
might be singing la la la la
before their nightcaps of grappa.

Couples down there are dancing
in the hotel ballroom as
the Sri Lankans in their apartment write home.

Pigeons, who today seemed sad, sleep.
Many things I've said my whole life were wrong.
The blackening air gets later, the moon rises red.

My camera on the windowsill for a long exposure.
Fragrance of rosemary hedge. Drapes.
I would not dream of shutting out this swarthy night.

Now I take off my nightgown,
I am sliding into the spacious sheets,
braced for terror.

*

I walked down by Frati, saw an old
basket shaped like a pack used for picking grapes.
A green snake flitted off its wicker top.

I went to the cellar once, saw
corked bottles, green and dark,
heavy with wine, mud

still on them, unlabeled, unwiped.
I found behind the villa
an herb garden,

asked the gardener his name, told him mine.
He seemed not to understand.
He seemed so far.

All across these gardens, so does everything.
This was day, but old night now has come—
drifts of girlish paralysis.

What would I do without my father?

In the limbs
of the tree,
I fear the past, look at the black

cypress out my window, at night
especially, all through it. Black
comes, stars streak above me,

the fishing town Pescallo immovable.
That's what I see.
The old fisherman there says, "I want that boy,"

wanting strength from a boy.
I want it too. The old man has
wooden bobbers, handmade sticks

in neon pinks, a blue, a green.
I will pile my hair high on my head
and slip them through.

When first I arrived in my bedroom,
I had been up all night on the plane,
had begun to bleed.

It picked up speed to an amazing
amount of red, I kept running
to the bathroom, there was

nothing I could think
to do. Red all over
that white tile expanse. Rose oriental
rug by my bed, red tapestry above,
full of rising roses.

*

Shaped like an upside down Y,
Lake Como was where I was,
at the crotch where the Y

comes together. Town,
Bellagio. The promontory there
steep. Up the Lake,

Alps. Separated from the town,
gates surround us,
we work on these formal grounds.

My mother was a painter—now, butterflies.

Men with scythes will hay the groves soon.
Yellow stars dash the sky.
The moon rises orange.

*

What is wrong with my feet?

Out the Gate
I gained height

on Pescallo,
the rain warm.

Legs wet,
shoes wet,
I stopped.
A garden plot seemed cared for.

I gazed below at the roofs,
remembered a man who threw
himself off one.
Was that the jingle of a tambourine?

Soaked, I approached
a boarded-up house,
got scared when I got near.
How old I've become, to turn away, I thought.

Another sound crossed the ground.
I thought *shoes, war,* looked down.

When the path sloped to a strange town,
I came to a gate locked shut.
To get out, I had to return
to where I heard the snake.

I ranged fast back up to Pescallo,
finally looked down on familiar
things—olive groves,
boats by docks.

When I came to where I had begun,
another gate was locked shut.

High all over was the wet green grass.
I walked through mud onto a steep wall
above the town,
"Aiuta!" I screamed for help.

A mutt looked up, didn't bark.
A couple wandered into the Square,
saw me up on the wall. They spoke
German, they
motioned
for me to jump.
I lunged

into the man's arms, watched
his hands around
my waist, ran

to my room, my bed, my body
swathed in heavy covers, the man's
hands had felt good. I tried
to sleep but could not.

Asleep now.
A blistering night, high in a plane,
A volcano—land cremating itself.
Disappearing features of a face—
no hills, no river, no mouth.

Fumes saturate nostrils cracked apart,
sour spit never leaves the mouth.
Absurd smoke shuts the air down
Lungs—gone.

*

The town church is grey.
Birds fly off its top into the white sky.

Each night I learn these hills by heart,
watch their faces darken.

Lights go off.
The hill to my right, an Alp

I've barely seen, it's chiseled like a European.
Far as I can see, no corn

grows anywhere here,
Hills come in close then recede—

those days, those months when my mother was dying.
I kept noticing a silo full of cow feed. Hills

everywhere here slant across one another. Some slam
down steep. A church could slide right off into the Lake.

Pennyroyal grows wild.
Red poppies in the weeds.

As if the night consents to a slow sexual speed,
elements here are breathing.

The ground breathes, the wind breathes,
how alive the earth still is.

For my Son, About to Be a Father

Making love last night with
my husband, not
your father, I thought how
sex is a lasting act.
I'm not talking about
genes, the long stream that
drips down from
one generation to
the next—we're all
in this together, it seems.

Federico Fellini's Birthday

Today, Mom, you would have been ninety and I
wonder what kind of old woman you
would have become because when you died
you were young.

I never knew til now that
you and Fellini shared
a birthday. You'd both be surprised
how the world's changed. Dad's okay.

His wife, who is younger than me by far, is
traveling soon to India and we, my husband
whom you barely knew and I, will stay
with Dad while she's away.

You'd be amazed how small
the world has become. There's so much
to say—I have grandchildren—for one.

If you could see Ruby Leah
named after you, you'd
die again, but this time
of happiness.

The Angel of Used Things

How to Read

Every day I read another
of your poems and sit in
the big chair here and watch
the sky turn orange as elsewhere, soon
I write a few words from your poem like
hell like *honey* like *say* and see what gives or
read another and write *mazurka*
which reminds me *duet* is good which makes me
write down *minuet*, then I think who's
watching the home fires, write down *pinch*,
look up *mazurka* only to find
right above is *mazuma*, a slang Yiddish word for "money."

Minuet is slow, a stately dance, then there's *whirl*
and *heaven* and *earth*, and *cogito ergo sum*.
I am so lost lately whirling heaven and earth
trying to right myself—*mazurka*—*mazurka*—
a lively Polish dance and it's above *mazy*, your daughter's name.

How to Daydream

Unplug the phone.
Don't check for messages.
Don't make a list of who you should call and chores.
Don't fret whether it's who or whom.
Was that a mouse? Don't put d-Con in the attic.
There's no bread in the house—forget about lunch.
Don't consider whether you'll get a chicken salad sandwich
at the bagel store.
Don't check your e-mail.
Don't, when you get an idea . . . oh forget it.
I just heard a bird singing.
Now I'm watching the trees blowing.
Is there supposed to be a thunderstorm?
Don't check the Weather Channel.
The other day I paid bills, made calls, cleared the decks.
This room is cold now—I'll turn the heat up.
Don't look up *daydreaming* to see what it makes you think of.
Meditation. Don't call a friend to find out
how to start meditating. Meditation Once
there was
a lost
soldier who
wandered into a
cathedral.
His cap on, he had crossed the
trolley tracks, walked along
a river. Music tugged at
him to go to a mikvah
to chant, and praise

the ammunition but a sign
said *Prohibited.*
I cannot tell you the time of day, nor what
the light was like, I cannot say whether it was
midmorning or late, or even what country it was.
I cannot even tell you that there was a beautiful beach there.

Contemporariness

No bear pie or stew in the new *Joy of Cooking*
nor porcupine, but in 94951, a California spa town,
a bakery's named *Bovine*.

No matchbook souvenirs from restaurants,
nor for that matter *Strike Anywheres*.

Now Dylan sings he sick of love,
and sheep after Dolly aren't the same.
Maybe they're sick of love as well.

In my town men are men—some things don't change.
One bragged he'd drink from the toilet bowl
rather than spend a dime on Evian.
Still I like the ursine kind.

Take whales.
Once killed for soap or oil or meat, then
we watched them from a boat—now that's about to go.
Whales are fragile it turns out and so's the ocean.

Books are cheap at amazon.com—it's bigger than the river, though
sidewinders in the desert still move in a looping sidewise motion.

Mercury

It's orange here as morning's light slips
through the juniper's blackish branches—the sun is far.
What's *silverado* I wonder and look it up but it's not there,
though *silvertongued* is and so is *quicksilver*,
another word for mercury—now the sun is higher.

On the dictionary's side, in pencil,
some boy wrote *I LOVE CHANTEE.*
Was his love the kind from afar or
had he kissed her the night before?
Who was the boy if a boy at all?

I examine the book for clues. Copyright 1973.
The computer screen and sky are blue—no matter
the story, it slips out from under. When I was five,
I begged the dentist for mercury. He gave me
a small container. Then one day I got a fever,
saw mercury rise wild in a thermometer.

Afterwards it was mercury for me
right above *mercy* in the dictionary—*mercury*
messenger god, god of thievery.

Past the Borderlands

Lone wolverines
roam your cold home
where you walk
through wind,
hills are gone.
You mark no fur, nor
shape, your dense
arms strong. Night
hones sheer
windows black, nor
sky, nor line, nor
land. Your day, in
these zones, verbless.

Arranging Books as Elegy

After you died, I fixed the garage up, moved
my desk and books out. Today I walked from shelf
to shelf, pulled out the books you wrote.

With stack in hand, I moved through the new place,
rubbing them—to say stroked would be more true.
How I rubbed your legs as your words went out.
Same spine—book, bone.

After I gathered your books, placed them on a shelf,
I walked again from shelf to shelf, picking books
you gave to me, or those admitted to our talk.

"Adam Bede," you once said. "Try that one first,"
(she's next to you now—she's close).
"George Eliot's my friend."

"Keats Keats! I don't want Keats and I don't know why."
You were telling me what you wanted read out back
when you died.

You wanted my Hopkins by your bed, wanted me to read him
in the yard, you said, when you went, and I did,
but where to put him, I'm confused.
At least for now though Keats is shelved far from you.

Uncle Sadness

How green goes
black under masses
of leaves, sadness
in the trees, how
the sun so startling
looks painted
by the masters.
With flat shadows,
it cuts
my neighbor's shed
in two.
Even shasta daisies
like stars in dew
bend from weather
and say
Say Uncle.

The Angel of Used Things

From Krakow to Tesuque, I move
through land and sea, sleep
by the Seine on newspapers,
my arms spread-eagled or shoved

inside my black wool devotionals.
I drift in and out of each shabby
Parisian, busy with their wares—
colanders, clogs or brass

barettes—my mouth goes dry.
When I found an arm in an
attic, I was not surprised.
The sun is shining as

I arrive by overnight
train, the navy sky studded
orange and free
above the speedaway shore.

Imagine this blue cotton
dress on my wife-to-be.
My money's in a brown paper
sandwich bag. Money puzzles me.

Throwing Away Books

Day one, day two, day three
of the long fall weekend
wore on as I flung tomes
all over the place,
pulled out books to keep,
made piles, letter *A* through letter *Z*.

I've always loved *Farenheit 451*:
now I know why. Those firemen's
job was, with books, to start fires.
This place is full of dry pyres.

Recipe for unadulterated guilt:
toss all borrowed books
lent by people who have died.
Gone *The Voice of Neurosis*.
Gone *Bike Tours of Holland*.

Now, what to do with my Harold Blooms
from the newest back to *The Anxiety of Influence*?
Most went—they all came back—some got saved.
I guess I'll give the rest away someday.

Unabashed, I heaved books hard
and fast across the room—
one of the finest physical activities known
to woman or man except for maybe sex.
Note *maybe*—that's how good it gets.

It's the molehill, not the mountain, influence I hate,
so out with the woe-is-me's and chuck the fall-flatters,
to the yawns and old farts, *mañana* I say.

Unfortunately, I could always find the above
because these were the books that never budged,
but my thin little Sappho kept jumping around—
now I don't have to fret, "Sappho, where
are you now?" She's there in the *S*'s easily found,
oh this great system, alphabetical order,
A before B, B before C—to be
an abecedarian—what a relief!

What a relief, not to worry who is next to whom—
that's how I once arranged my books.
Usually Tess Gallagher was next to Ray Carver—
—then after he died, I always made sure—
and Clampitt loved Hopkins so I kept them together.
The whole thing got tiring and it was hard to find books.

Jettison great books reccommended by friends
that I tried to read but—my problem—could not.
There are lots.
Or, put it this way, were.
Gone *My First American*.
Gone *The Divine Woman*.

When my eyes fell on the C's
and I saw the Hart Cranes
I nearly swooned, I kid you not,
I want to be surrounded by mountains like these.
Gertrude Stein has a whole shelf and Dante too,

and Ammons, A.R. and Stafford, Bill—
my early guide, my midwestern Virgil.
Double *Lovers* (Duras) and double Calvinos,
and two *The Travels of Marco Polo.*

What about well-heeled books, what about snobbishness?
I chucked Random House books and books from Knopf,
Houghton-Mifflin, Norton and Atheneum,
but one tiny tome, *I Have No Clue,*
a beaut by Jack Wiler published by who-knows-who
would never find its way to the heap.
Now Wiler's there between Wilbur and Williams.

Once I bought a fat book, *Self-Publishing,*
perused it, squirreled it away.
I didn't *squirrel* it away—I hid it in shame!
Now put it out near *How to Market Your Book.*
"Give it its due," I say.

And books by friends I love
as much as their books.
Listen to the end of *Charlotte's Web:*
It is not often that someone comes along
who is a true friend and a good writer.
Charlotte was both.

What luck to have Charlottes, a blessing in life.
But what about those folks you dislike?
What if you like, even love, what they wrote?

I'll keep the poet I think's a creep.
He's been rude to my friend and ruder to me.

When I started to toss, it was almost too much—
awash in each book—then I got tough.
Who's a goner? Who is not?

Gone *The History of Hadassah*,
hasta luego my Pavese novels.
Verga gone, and Tasso too,
finitto my study of Italian many moons ago, blue.

Gone *Art and Psychoanalysis*,
gone *Art and Physics*—but
to place Hawking's biography near Giacometti's,
is heavenly—
Isadora Duncan, FDR and Max Kaminsky
used to live yon and hither,
now the biogs huddle together.

Selma Fraiberg—bon voyage
most of Freud too,
Walter Pater—a gem I'd never toss—
but what of Roland Barthes?
He's in the heap with the finest of folks.
After much thought,
out went Tennyson and Browning too.
How could you, you ask? Answer:
the web and anthologies, plus
I live near the library.
But it's more complex though.
Never would I heave Catullus or Chaucer.
Never would I part with the sonnets of Shakespeare.

Gone *Memory and Forgetting* by some famous philosopher,
and even though my daughter-in-law's mother's
a Jungian analyst,
now it's time for Dr. Carl and I to say aloha.

Do I need three dictionaries of slang?
Do I need books I'll never crack on the Yiddish lang?
As other people threw them away,
I rescued them one by one, but for that job—
find someone else, I say!

Moliére? Sorry Frenchie,
you've been with me since high school,
that's long enough.
Corneille and Racine got pitched years ago.
Ou sont les neiges d'antan? Villon?
Adored him then, adore him still.

Books carry weight,
that's for sure.
That's how this began
at the start but
I need the space for
my anxiety of influence
to reek havoc
if it wants,
however it goes—
art is art.

I like being here
with pages
that gleam—

the books
for now
anyway—
A to Z.

Like river
like sea
like ocean
like stream—
oh Hart Crane
stick with me
as I make my way out
early, to
see what comes.

Dedications

The Cradle * for Aquila Chase-Daniel, on the occasion of your birth

Holy Wall * for Mother Mary John of West Malling Abbey

Beach Rubble * for Flicka and Jane Gatti Rodman, in memory

No Noise Now * for Michael and Leslie Bissaillon

How to Read * for Baron Wormser, on reading *Mulroney & Others*

Arranging Books as Elegy * for Amy Clampitt, in memory

Notes

The Cradle was inspired by Elaine de Kooning's "Cave Painting."

The Book of Crime * "How much I would have bartered" is from Hart Crane's *Repose of Rivers*.

Unpacking * *Struwwelpeter* is a collection of nineteenth-century German cautionary verse tales by Heinrich Hoffman.

And Then I Talked to a Salamander * "Dark woods" refers to the second line of the opening stanza of Dante's *Inferno: mi ritrovai per una selva oscura*, "I found myself astray in a dark wood."

Other Books in the
Notable Voices Series

CavanKerry's Mission

Through publishing and programming, CavanKerry Press connects communities of writers with communities of readers. We publish poetry that reaches from the page to include the reader, by the finest new and established contemporary writers. Our programming brings our books and our poets to people where they live, cultivating new audiences and nourishing established ones.